This Handwriting Notebook Belongs To:

A is For

B

B is For

C is For

D

D is For

E is For

F is For

G

G is For

H is For

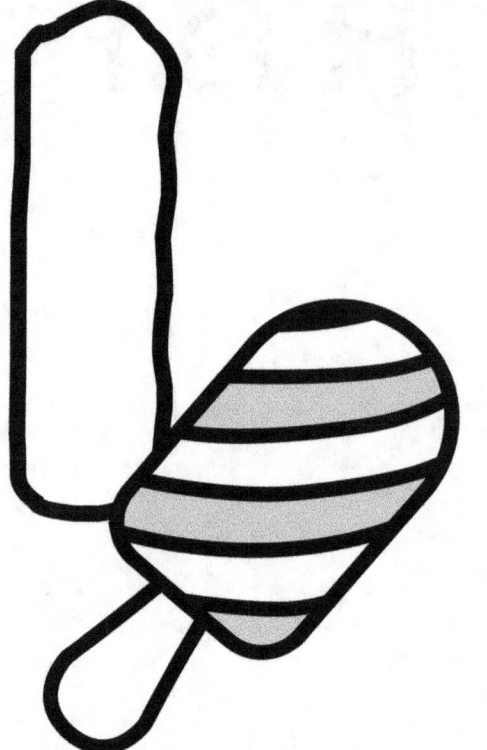

I

I is For

J

J is For

K

K is For

L is For

M is For

N is For

O is For

P

P is For

Q is For

R

R is For

s

S is For

T is For

U is For

V

V is For

W is For

x

X is For

Y

Y is For

z

Z is For